THE STORY OF THE
CASTLE

Written by Miriam Moss
Illustrated by Chris Forsey

SIMON & SCHUSTER
YOUNG BOOKS

First published in 1993 by
Simon & Schuster Young Books
Simon & Schuster Limited
Campus 400
Maylands Avenue
Hemel Hempstead
Hertfordshire HP2 7EZ

Planned and produced by
Andromeda Oxford Limited
11-15 The Vineyard
Abingdon
Oxon OX14 3PX

ISBN 0-7500-1454-7
Printed in Singapore

Foreword

The best way to avoid being attacked is to live somewhere which is difficult for people to reach. In ancient times, people built their homes on isolated rocky headlands, dangerous cliff edges and high, flat-topped hills. Obstacles such as walls were gradually added to make invading the settlements even more difficult.

The word 'castle' means a building with massive defences. This might be an ancient fortress or a large house with battlements. Some castles were magnificent homes, with great feasting halls, grand chambers, large kitchens and their own private chapels.

Castle life was a constant preparation for war. Attackers used powerful catapults to hurl missiles. The castle archers fired crossbows at the enemy, through the castle's slit-like windows. If the attackers managed to get inside the castle, people fought with swords, axes and maces. The development of gunpowder meant that castles were no longer able to withstand being bombarded. Their usefulness had come to an end.

Many of the ancient castles we visit today seem empty and silent. But in their day they were noisy, bustling colourful places as you will find out.

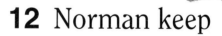

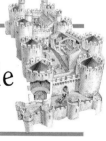

Contents

Bronze Age citadel

4 The royal tombs were built into the hillside. They consisted of long passages, with chambers cut out of the rock at the ends.

5 The palace was finely decorated. The walls were covered with frescoes. The floors were first covered in plaster, then divided into squares and decorated.

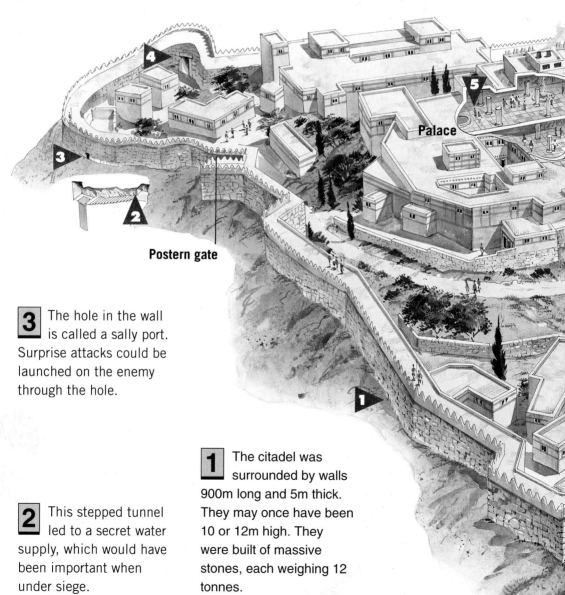

Palace

Postern gate

3 The hole in the wall is called a sally port. Surprise attacks could be launched on the enemy through the hole.

1 The citadel was surrounded by walls 900m long and 5m thick. They may once have been 10 or 12m high. They were built of massive stones, each weighing 12 tonnes.

2 This stepped tunnel led to a secret water supply, which would have been important when under siege.

6 The Lion Gate marks the entrance to the citadel. The approach to the gate runs between two guarded walls. This meant that an enemy would come under attack before reaching the gate.

Mycenae is the most famous Bronze Age citadel in Greece. Built on a rocky hilltop, it lies half hidden by deep ravines and a rampart. In the 13th century BC, Mycenae was the citadel of King Agamemnon. His court was famous for its fabulous wealth.

In the 19th century, archaeologists began to excavate (dig up) the royal tombs at Mycenae. They found a hoard of golden treasures, including vases and face masks, and swords with golden hilts (handles).

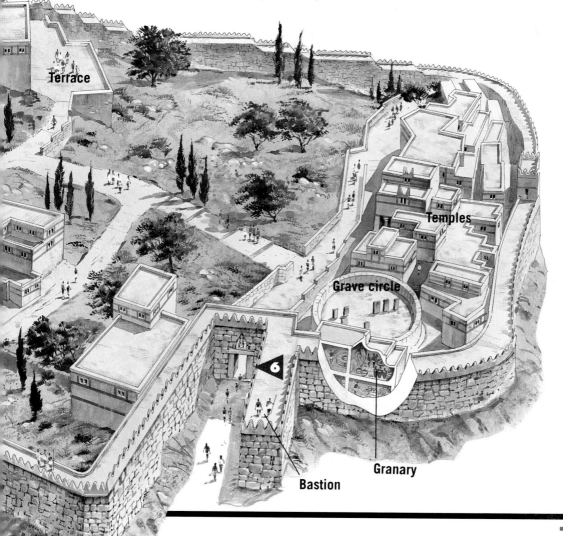

Terrace

Temples

Grave circle

Bastion

Granary

Iron Age hill fort

Cadbury Castle was an Iron Age hill fort in Somerset, England. It was attacked by the Romans in about AD 60 and its Celtic inhabitants massacred. By around AD 500, however, Cadbury had become one of the largest, strongest forts in England.

Legend says that it was the site of Camelot – the court of King Arthur and the famous Knights of the Round Table. The last time Cadbury was occupied was by the Saxon king, Ethelred II, from AD 1009–1019. He defended it against attack by the Danes.

A steep hill became harder for an enemy to climb if banks and ditches were dug around the sides. A bank was built, then a ditch and then a steep slope, which the attackers would have to cross to reach the castle. All this time, the defenders could use their weapons on the attackers.

3 The hill had four or five lines of Iron Age banks and ditches which attackers found very difficult to get past.

2 The entrance passage was lined with stone and had a single guard chamber above. Feet, hooves and wheels have worn the rock path into a hollow over 1.8m deep.

4 After the Roman massacre, the defenders were left unburied. Their bodies were probably torn apart by wolves. Brooches have been found inside the gate, as well as over 100 iron weapons and scattered bones.

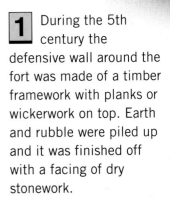

1 During the 5th century the defensive wall around the fort was made of a timber framework with planks or wickerwork on top. Earth and rubble were piled up and it was finished off with a facing of dry stonework.

Rampart

5 The large feasting hall had a thatched roof and timber frame, filled with wattle and daub. Part of the hall was divided off as a private chamber.

Southwest gate tower

6 This is one of three, probably military, rectangular buildings which have been excavated at Cadbury.

►Jewish fort

Masada stands on an outcrop of rock high above the desert overlooking the Dead Sea in Israel. It was developed by Herod the Great. In AD 73, a group of 960 Jews used Masada as their base while they battled for freedom from Roman rule.

One night, the leader of the Jews persuaded his people to end their own lives rather than be taken prisoner. Each man had to kill his own family, 10 men were chosen by lots to kill the rest, and the last remaining man had to set fire to the palace and then kill himself. When the Romans reached Masada the next day they were met with a terrible silence.

1 King Herod the Great built a palace for himself on three levels, with terraces overlooking the Dead Sea.

2 The casemate wall surrounding the fortress had many towers as an additional defence. Inside the wall were 110 rooms.

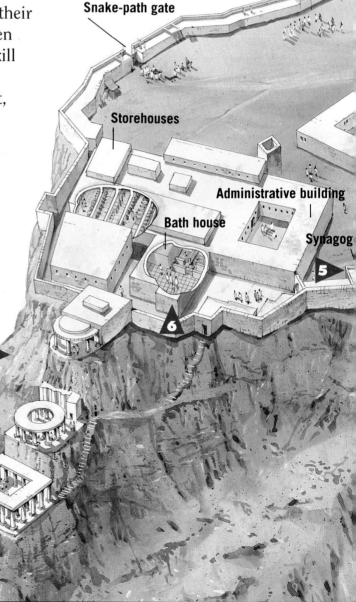

Snake-path gate

Storehouses

Bath house

Administrative building

Synagog

3 The huge underground water cisterns were filled by rainwater. Two Jewish women and five children hid in the cisterns to escape from the Romans. They were the only survivors.

4 King Herod's western palace had a throne room which was decorated with a beautiful, multi-coloured mosaic. Part of this mosaic can still be seen today.

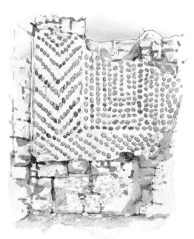

This synagogue wall was decorated with unusual designs made from small stones and pieces of pottery.

6 The ritual Jewish bath had a main pool and two small pools. One small pool collected water for the main pool. The other small pool was for bathers to wash their hands and feet before entering the main pool.

5 Two parchment scrolls, from the Hebrew Bible, were found buried under the synagogue floor. They may have been hidden there by the Jews before they died.

Norman keep

The castle at Rochester, England, is a good example of a Norman square keep. During the 11th and 12th centuries, the Normans (who came from France) occupied England and built many castles as strongholds. The castle served not only as a fortress, but also as a home for its lord, a court and a prison.

Rochester was one of the first English castles to be fortified with stone, in place of timber. In 1215 it was defended against King John for seven weeks, despite being battered by stone-throwing machines and the fat of 40 pigs being used to set fire to the keep.

3 The semicircular tower was built after the siege in 1215. Its curved wall was designed to deflect missiles away from the castle walls.

2 The forebuilding protected the entrance. Visitors had to pass through a small lobby, a guard tower and a portcullis.

Mural tower

1 The outer bailey was used for sports contests. It also housed all the people who worked in the castle.

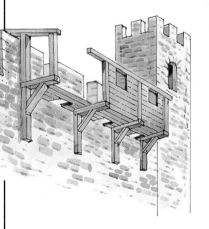

The hoarding was a wooden gallery which was attached to the top of the outer wall of the castle when it was under attack. The hoarding was held up by timber beams. It was used as a platform from which the defenders could drop heavy objects on the attackers below.

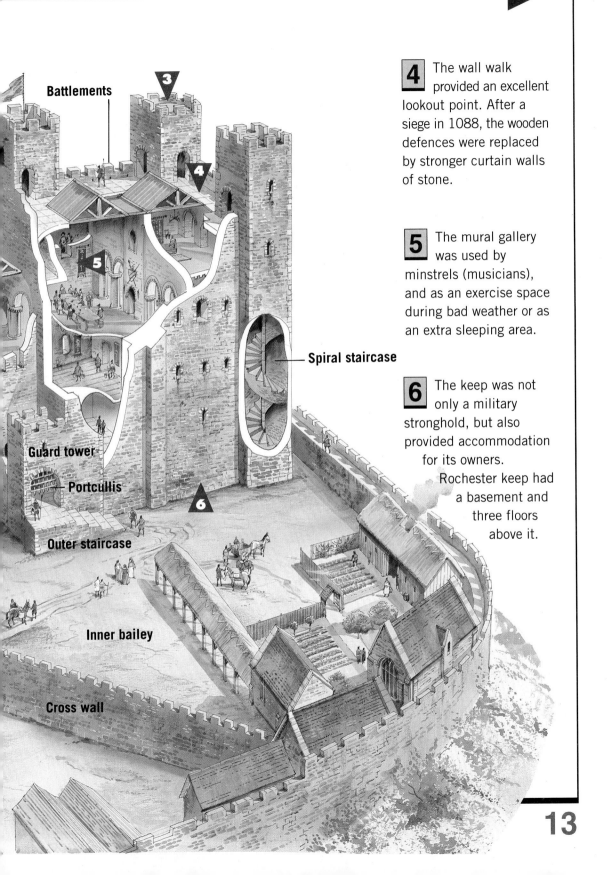

Battlements

3

4

5

Spiral staircase

Guard tower

Portcullis

Outer staircase

6

Inner bailey

Cross wall

4 The wall walk provided an excellent lookout point. After a siege in 1088, the wooden defences were replaced by stronger curtain walls of stone.

5 The mural gallery was used by minstrels (musicians), and as an exercise space during bad weather or as an extra sleeping area.

6 The keep was not only a military stronghold, but also provided accommodation for its owners. Rochester keep had a basement and three floors above it.

► Crusader castle

Krak des Chevaliers, in Syria, was built in 1170 by the Crusaders. They were fighting the Muslims for control of Jerusalem and the Holy Land. The castle was vitally important because it lay in the only mountain pass that was open all year round.

The castle's gigantic towers were made of massive stone blocks. There was a strong keep, with walls 8.5m thick in places. The Great Hall was used for meetings of the Chapter of the Hospitallers – the Crusader knights who governed Krak. The castle also contained a storeroom which could hold enough food to feed the garrison for five years.

1 The entrance to the castle included a long passage, with guard rooms on either side opening onto a hidden moat between the inner and outer walls.

2 The Hall of Massive Pillars lay on the side of the courtyard. It contained kitchens, dining rooms and storerooms.

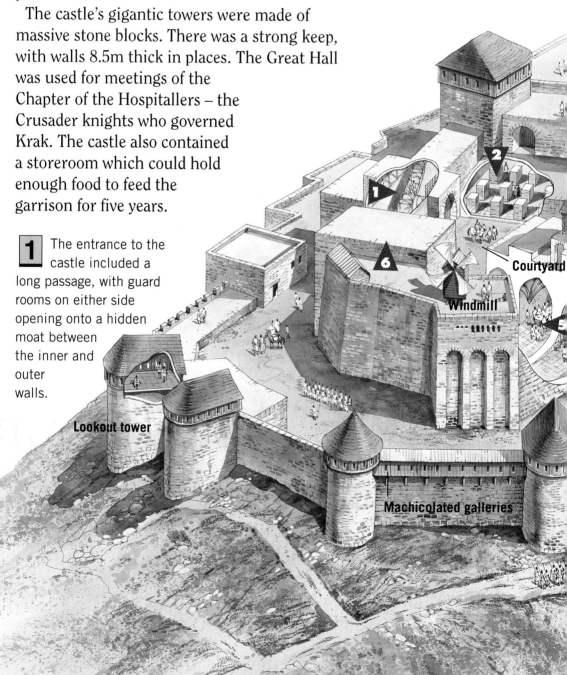

Courtyard

Windmill

Lookout tower

Machicolated galleries

3 A square tower jutted out from the outer rampart. It defended the narrow bridge of the aqueduct which supplied the moat with water.

4 The 'One Hundred and Twenty Metre Hall' contained a well and four bread ovens. It was also used as a warehouse. Toilets were built into the north wall.

5 The Great Hall was 27m long and 7.5m wide. It had a pointed, arched roof.

6 A Crusader chapel was built into the rampart. It was converted into a mosque when the Muslims captured Krak.

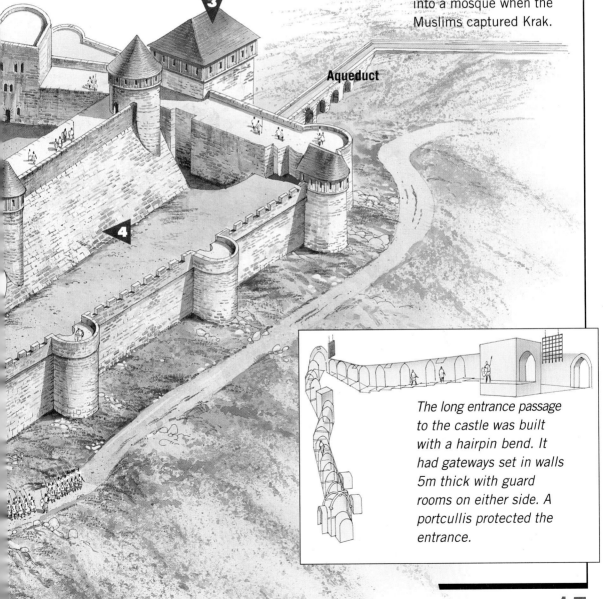

Aqueduct

The long entrance passage to the castle was built with a hairpin bend. It had gateways set in walls 5m thick with guard rooms on either side. A portcullis protected the entrance.

13th century castle

Conwy Castle, in North Wales, was built by Edward I. It was one of several new castles built to help him conquer Wales. Edward I was a well-travelled, experienced soldier. He knew that the corners on the old square keeps were blindspots which meant they could easily be undermined by the enemy. So he built Conwy in a narrow rectangular shape, defended by eight strong round towers.

Conwy was designed in two parts, one for the King, arranged like a castle within a castle which could be separately defended, and the other for the garrison overlooking the town. The building materials often had to be carried long distances yet it took just four years to complete Conwy Castle, from 1283 to 1287. In those days the walls were whitewashed so that the castle stood out as a shining symbol of royal power to all who saw it.

Chapel tower

Stockhouse tower

Kitchen tow

North tow

Drawbridge

3 The King's tower was one of eight huge towers around the castle wall. These were used for defence, and also for accommodation.

2 The walled town was built at the same time as the castle. The townspeople were protected not only by the wall but also by the castle and its defences.

1 Loopholes were slit-like or cross-shaped openings in the castle wall. Archers could fire their arrows through them, safe from attack.

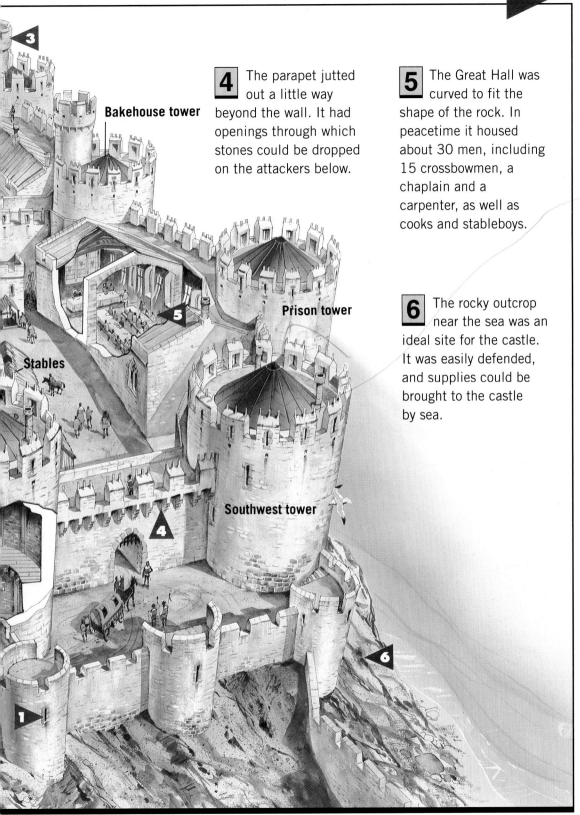

Bakehouse tower

4 The parapet jutted out a little way beyond the wall. It had openings through which stones could be dropped on the attackers below.

5 The Great Hall was curved to fit the shape of the rock. In peacetime it housed about 30 men, including 15 crossbowmen, a chaplain and a carpenter, as well as cooks and stableboys.

Prison tower

Stables

6 The rocky outcrop near the sea was an ideal site for the castle. It was easily defended, and supplies could be brought to the castle by sea.

Southwest tower

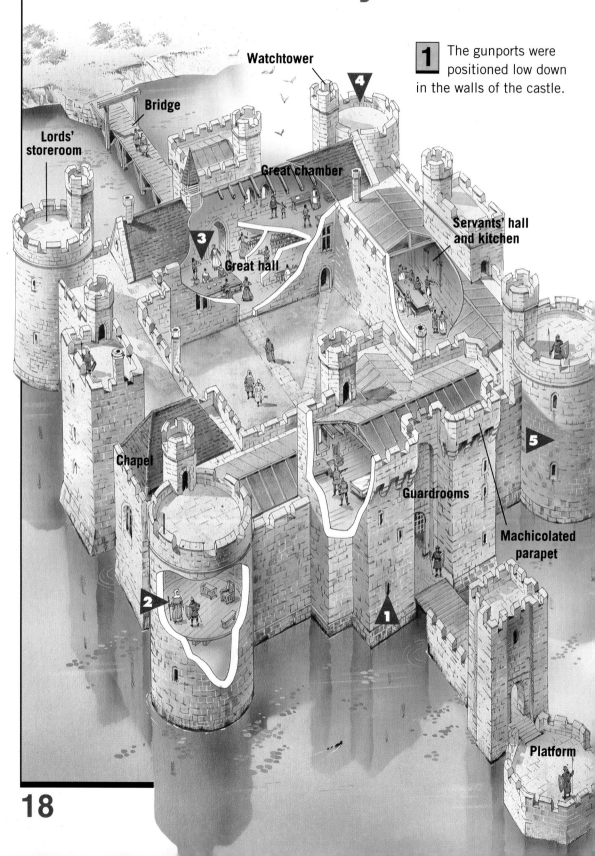

Watchtower

Bridge

Lords' storeroom

1 The gunports were positioned low down in the walls of the castle.

Great chamber

Servants' hall and kitchen

Great hall

Chapel

Guardrooms

Machicolated parapet

Platform

2 There were plenty of rooms for guests in the little chambers in the gatehouses and turrets.

3 Sir Edward's grand private rooms were away from the servants' quarters. He lived in style with different rooms for formal or family occasions.

4 The castle had a pigeon loft of 300 nests. The pigeons provided meat, and feathers for mattresses and cushions.

5 The living quarters were protected by a moat and huge, round towers. The gatehouse and rear entrance tower had machicolations around the top.

Bodiam Castle was one of the last castles to be built in England. It was the result of centuries of experience in castle design and a good example of a castle which was built for defence but which was also a comfortable home.

In the 14th century, the French attacked several of the English ports along the south coast. As a result, the coastal defences had to be made stronger. In 1386, a rich knight, Sir Edward Dalyngrigge, was given a royal licence to fortify his manor house at Bodiam in Sussex. It became Bodiam Castle. Firearms were now being used for defence, and Bodiam was one of the first castles to have gunports.

6 The wide moat was crossed by a bridge at right angles to the main approach. On that bridge, the invaders could be attacked from the side, making a wider target. The postern (rear) gate also had defences. These were similar to those at the front.

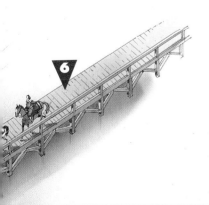

The gatehouse had keyhole gunports. The primitive guns were shaped like a tube and could be poked through the round hole. The gunner could look through the slit above to take aim.

French château

3 Chambord had an elaborate skyline of towers and turrets. They were a strange mixture of French and Italian architectural styles.

In the 16th century, François I, the King of France, decided to build a splendid new castle, or château, on the bank of the River Loire at Chambord. A hunting lodge had originally stood on the site. The château of Chambord was designed by the Italian architect, Domenico da Cortona. It was a huge project.

Some 1,800 men worked under three master

2 The château had 400 rooms – private chambers for the King and his family, guest rooms, audience chambers, dining rooms and kitchens.

1 In the centre of the castle there was a huge spiral staircase. Two people could climb up it without ever meeting. Two ramps twisted and turned one above the other.

masons. These three men are thought to have changed the architect's original plans. They created the extraordinary mixture of plain and decorative styles found at Chambord. The château was designed along the lines of a fortified castle. The massive keep, corner towers, moat and cannon openings in the battlements are all features more usually found in a castle.

4 The château was begun in 1519. It took many years to complete. The final detail – the gilded lead roof of the keep – was completed in 1546.

6 The terrace had projecting stones, called corbels. These were designed for cannons, although they were never used for this purpose.

5 The castle had a wide moat. Entry was across the moat by a bridge facing the keep.

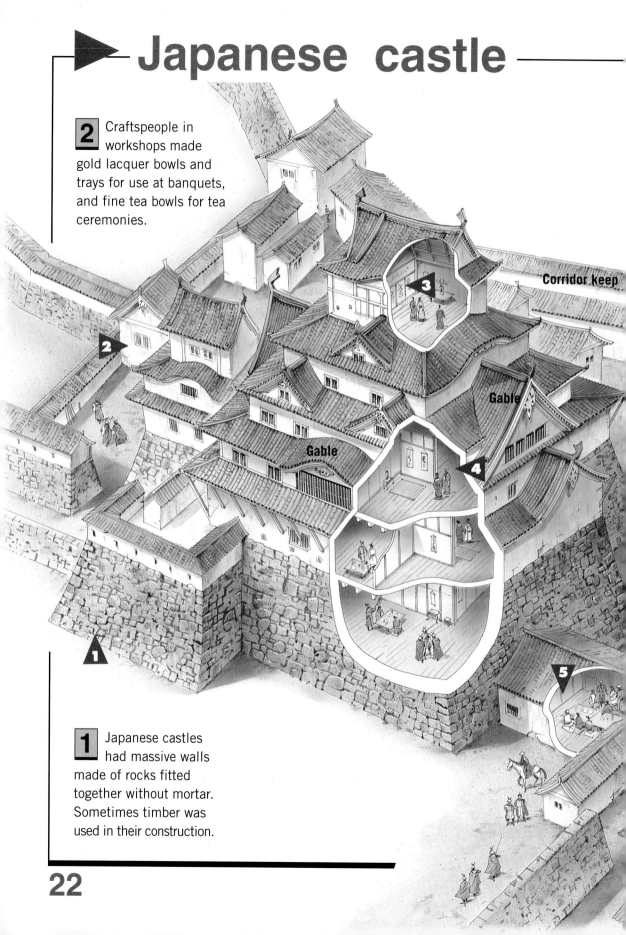

2 Craftspeople in workshops made gold lacquer bowls and trays for use at banquets, and fine tea bowls for tea ceremonies.

Corridor keep

Gable

Gable

1 Japanese castles had massive walls made of rocks fitted together without mortar. Sometimes timber was used in their construction.

3 The walls, ceilings and screens were painted with beautiful scenes from nature. The painters used bright colours and gold leaf.

Many castles were built in Japan from 1568 to 1600 by powerful, military warlords. The castles' grand architecture and rich interiors were signs of the status and authority of the warlords. They constantly battled with each other.

The finest surviving castle of this period is Himeji-jo ('jo' means 'castle' in Japanese). The original building dated from the 14th century. It was enlarged by Hideyoshi, a military leader and master of siege warfare, who took possession of it in 1577. Himeji was given its present, majestic appearance in about 1600 by Ikeda Terumasa, another important military leader.

4 The central compound contained the donjon (keep). Japanese castles were unusual in having decorated gables (sloping ends of a pitched roof). Three smaller donjons were clustered around the main building.

5 The castle compound included the living quarters for the soldiers and servants of the powerful lord. The castle was the centre for trade, finance, learning and the arts.

6 Loopholes in the wall were used for defence. Arrows or muskets were fired through the holes at the enemy.

4 The Diwan-i-Khas (Hall of Private Audience) was the most luxurious of the fort's buildings. At each end of the hall was written in gold: 'If on earth there is a paradise, then this is it, yes this is it, this is it.'

In 1628 Shah Jahan became Emperor of India. He decided to move his capital from Agra to Delhi. In 1638, he began planning his new city. Inside the city, he built a great fortified citadel containing a royal palace called the Red Fort, after the deep-red colour of its 30m-high sandstone walls.

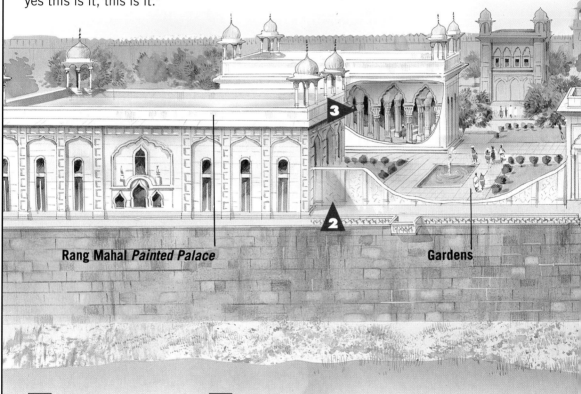

Rang Mahal *Painted Palace*

Gardens

3 The Diwan-i-Am (Hall of Public Audience) is made up of many arches. The red sandstone used for these buildings was covered by a fine white plaster which was polished to look like marble.

2 Balustrades and screens of marble, which looked like fine lace, protected the beautiful gardens. A canal called the Canal of Paradise supplied water for the fountains and pools.

1 Each morning, the Emperor inspected newly captured elephants. The elephants were scrubbed clean and painted black and then covered with embroidered cloth and silver bells.

The Emperor's architects were famous for their beautiful buildings. Inside the palace enclosure were decorated pavilions, marble palaces, courtyards and galleries with carved archways, marble floors and high, domed ceilings. Many were decorated with gold and silver and precious stones.

5 The famous Peacock Throne stood in the Diwan-i-Khas on a huge marble slab. A gold canopy on pillars sparkling with emeralds covered the throne.

Lahore gate

Moti Masjid *Pearl Mosque*

6 Hundreds of people were employed inside the fort, for example, bakers, torch makers, perfume makers and goldsmiths.

In the 19th century, a dispute about slavery led to the southern states of the USA leaving the Union of States and becoming the Confederate States of America. The northern states formed the Federal Union of States.

Fort Sumter in South Carolina faced a dilemma. It was a Federal fort in the middle of Confederate territory. The small garrison of 10 officers and 73 men was under the command of Major Robert Anderson. The governor of South Carolina ordered Major Anderson to surrender. He refused and thousands of Confederate troops surrounded the fort. They bombarded the fort with mortar shells. The fort was set ablaze. The American Civil War had begun.

2 Only one life was lost at Fort Sumter after the final surrender. When Major Anderson fired his last salute, a charge of gunpowder exploded and killed a gunner.

Building ma

Stair tower

1 Fort Sumter was a five-sided strong-hold made from brick. It stood on an island in Charleston harbour, South Carolina.

3 The fort was designed for a garrison of 650 men. There were provisions for 135 guns, arranged in tiers around the walls of the fort. The middle tier was never finished, and guns were placed only in the top and bottom tiers.

4 In 1865, the Confederate troops abandoned the fort. The (now) Major General Anderson returned on the anniversary of his departure to raise the same flag he had lowered four years before.

Major Robert Anderson's courage in defending the fort in April 1861 made him famous in American history.

Officers' quarters

Lantern

Sand

Soldiers' barracks

6 The walls of the fort were 1.5-3m thick and rose 12m above the water.

5 The position of the fort on an island at the mouth of the harbour meant it could defend a wide range of territory, both on land and at sea.

Romantic castle

Castles gradually stopped being used for defence, but people continued to build them to show off their wealth and importance. Rich people also built castles for nostalgic or romantic reasons, as they still do today.

'Mad' King Ludwig II started building his romantic castle, Neuschwanstein, in 1869. It stands high up in the mountains of Bavaria in southern Germany. Ludwig became King when he was only 18 years old. He was shy and felt misunderstood by the world around him. He decided to shut himself away and surround himself with beautiful things. Instead of an architect, he hired a theatre-set designer to build Neuschwanstein.

Neuschwanstein was the favourite castle of the lonely King Ludwig II of Bavaria. The King loved the music written by Wagner, especially the opera 'Lohengrin' in which the swan plays an important part.

2 In the King's bedroom on 12 June 1886, Ludwig's enemies declared him insane. Ludwig died mysteriously the next day. He and his doctor had gone for a walk and were found dead in a lake.

1 Huge amounts of materials were needed to build the castle. They were pulled up the mountain by a steam-operated crane. In one year 472 tonnes of marble, 1,581 tonnes of sandstone and 400,000 bricks were used.

3 Ludwig had six paintings of saintly past kings hung in his throne room. They were meant to show his belief in the religious connection between kings and God.

4 The name Neuschwanstein means 'new swan stone'. There was a swan in one form or another in almost every room in the castle. The swan was a symbol of purity and the King's favourite creature.

5 The King had a grotto full of stalactites built between the living room and the study. The stalactites were made of plaster of Paris.

6 The castle employed hundreds of people from the villages around it. For almost 20 years, they made their living from the building of the castle.

Spiral staircase

Courtyard

Gatehouse

Glossary

Aqueduct
A bridge which carries water.

Archaeologist
A person who studies the remains left by life in the past.

Bailey
The outer court of a castle which could be defended from attack. There was sometimes an outer bailey and an inner bailey.

Balustrade
An ornamental rail.

Barbican
An outer enclosure in front of the main gate of the castle.

Bastion
A fortified stone wall.

Battlements
A low structure built on a wall for defence or decoration.

Breach
To break through.

Bronze Age
The period of history which in Ancient Greece lasted from about 2,000–1,000 BC.

Casemate wall
A fortified wall on which guns were often mounted.

Château
A manor house, especially in France.

Cistern
A tank for storing water, sometimes underground.

Citadel
A stronghold inside or close to a city, or any strongly fortified building or refuge.

Corbel
A stone or timber jutting out from a wall to support the end of a beam or a platform.

Crenellations
Stone battlements jutting out of the castle walls.

Curtain wall
The wall which enclosed a castle courtyard.

Donjon
The medieval word for the keep of a castle.

Embrasure
An opening in a wall or parapet.

Forebuilding
A building which protected the entrance to a castle.

Fresco
A painting done in water colours on wet plaster.

Garrison
The place where troops are stationed to guard a fortified building.

Gilded
Covered in gold or a substance looking like gold.

Hoarding
A timber gallery built at the top of a wall or tower.

Iron Age
The traditional name given to a time when smelting and use of iron was widespread. It followed the Bronze Age.

Keep
The main tower of a castle – often able to defend itself without outside help.

Lintel
The flat top of a door or window opening.

Loophole
A slit or cross-shaped opening in a castle wall, through which archers fired their arrows.

Machicolation
An overhanging parapet or fighting gallery through which missiles could be dropped.

Mason
A person skilled in working in and building with stone.

Moat
A deep ditch around a castle, usually filled with water.

Mortar
Cannon with a short barrel.

Mosaic
A design or decoration made of small pieces of glass, pottery or stone.

Mosque
A Muslim place of worship.

Motte and bailey
The bailey was a timber tower which stood on top of a large mound of earth, called the motte.

Nostalgic
When someone longs for the past.

Parapet
A wall to protect a castle and its soldiers.

Pavilion
An open, ornamental building or decorative shelter.

Petition
A formal request to an authority, such as the king or emperor.

Portcullis
A grille which slides up and down in grooves cut in the stones of a gate passage.

Postern
A rear gate.

Privy
A small lavatory.

Rampart
The embankment surrounding a fort, including any walls built for defence.

Refectory
A dining hall.

Rock-cut
A tomb or cave carved from solid rock.

Sally port
A hidden entrance from which defenders could mount a surprise attack on invaders.

Scroll
A roll of parchment used for writing on.

Siege
An operation carried out to capture a fortified place by surrounding it and not allowing people in or out.

Synagogue
A building for Jewish religious services.

Turret
A small tower.

Undermine
To tunnel or dig under a building so it gradually gets weaker.

Vault
An underground passage or room, often used for storage.

Wattle and daub
A way of making walls from woven twigs plastered with a mixture of clay, wood and sometimes chopped straw.

Index